Wild Weather

TORNADO

Heinemann
LIBRARY

Catherine Chambers

www.heinemann.co.uk/library

Visit our website to find out more information about **Heinemann Library** books.

To order:

 Phone ++44 (0)1865 888066

 Send a fax to ++44 (0)1865 314091

 Visit the Heinemann Bookshop at www.heinemann.co.uk/library to browse our catalogue and order online.

First published in Great Britain by Heinemann Library, Halley Court, Jordan Hill, Oxford OX2 8EJ, a division of Reed Educational and Professional Publishing Ltd. Heinemann is a registered trademark of Reed Educational & Professional Publishing Ltd.

OXFORD MELBOURNE AUCKLAND JOHANNESBURG BLANTYRE
GABORONE IBADAN PORTSMOUTH NH (USA) CHICAGO

Designed by Visual Image
Illustration by Paul Bale
Originated by Ambassador Litho Ltd.
Printed and bound in South China.

ISBN 0 431 15060 5

06 05 04 03 02
10 9 8 7 6 5 4 3 2 1

British Library Cataloguing in Publication Data

Chambers, Catherine
Tornado. – (Wild Weather)
1. Tornadoes – Juvenile literature
I. Title
551.5'53
ISBN 0431150605

Acknowledgements

The Publishers would like to thank the following for permission to reproduce photographs: Associated Press pp8, 14, 19, 20, 23, 27, 28, Corbis pp21, 25, FLPA p22, Oxford Scientific Films pp4, 11, 15, PA Photos p26, Photodisc p16, Rex Features p12, Robert Harding Picture Library p5, Science Photo Library pp10, 13, 18, Stone pp7, 9, 17, 24, 29.

Cover photograph reproduced with permission of Imagestate.

The Publishers would like to thank the Met Office for their assistance with the preparation of this book.

Every effort has been made to contact copyright holders of any material reproduced in this book. Any omissions will be rectified in subsequent printings if notice is given to the Publisher.

Any words appearing in the text in bold, **like this**, are explained in the Glossary.

Contents

What is a tornado?

A tornado is a moving, spinning **funnel** of wind. It swirls from a dark, towering cloud. The wind in a tornado is very strong. The tornado can suck up anything in its path.

The spinning wind throws everything out at the sides as it moves along. This makes a huge cloud of dust and **debris** around the tornado.

Where do tornadoes happen?

Tornadoes can happen in most places. This map shows some parts of the world where tornadoes happen. There are many tornadoes in the USA.

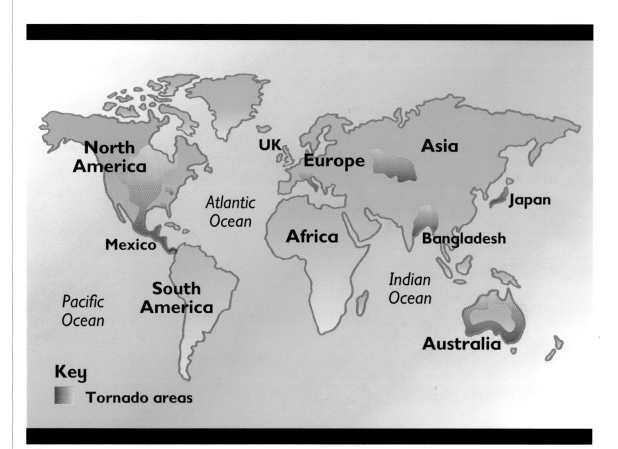

North America

UK

Europe

Asia

Japan

Atlantic Ocean

Mexico

Africa

Bangladesh

Indian Ocean

Pacific Ocean

South America

Australia

Key

Tornado areas

This part of the United States lies in an area called Tornado Alley. It has more tornadoes than anywhere else in the world.

Wind and cloud

Wind is made when **masses** of air move around. Some masses are cold. Others are warm. Warm air usually rises. Cold air rushes in to fill the space it leaves. This causes strong winds.

Water vapour is always in the air. When millions of droplets of water vapour become cold they form clouds. Tornadoes come from storm clouds. This picture of clouds was taken from space.

Why do tornadoes happen?

Tornadoes happen in hot, moist weather. Heavy storm clouds form. They suck up warm, moist air from below. Cool air blows across the top of the cloud. These movements make a twisting wind.

The spinning wind makes a cone shaped **funnel**
that can dip right down to the ground.
Sometimes tornadoes move over water. This
makes a **waterspout**.

What are tornadoes like?

People can see most tornadoes coming. They can also see dust and **debris** swirling around the bottom of the **funnel**. Yet no one knows exactly where the tornado will go.

Tornadoes often happen as part of
thunderstorms. People see lightning and hear
thunder. Heavy rain falls.

Harmful tornadoes

The winds in tornadoes travel faster than any other winds. Tornadoes only affect a narrow area. They destroy anything in their path.

Dark tornado clouds can hold **masses** of icy
hailstones. The hailstones fall and sometimes
hurt people and animals. They can also damage
buildings and **crops**.

Tornado Alley

Oklahoma is in the middle of the United States. It is part of Tornado Alley. A lot of damaging tornadoes happen here.

Terrible tornadoes hit Oklahoma on 3 May 1999. They sucked up and threw out everything in their paths. The flying **debris** hit people and buildings – 45 people were killed.

Preparing for the tornado

Weather forecasters tell **emergency services** when a tornado has formed. The emergency services use radio, television and the Internet to warn people about the tornado.

Storm-chasers are people who try to get close to tornadoes. The storm-chasers take pictures of the tornadoes. They also warn weather forecasters that a tornado is coming.

Tornado warning

On 3 April 1974 **weather forecasters** in the United States knew that many tornadoes were coming. They sent out over 160 tornado warnings to 14 **states**.

On that day, 148 tornadoes struck. Over 300
people were killed and over 30,000 buildings
were destroyed. No one could stop the
tornadoes.

Coping with tornadoes

Tornadoes can damage all types of buildings. In some places, people are able to go to specially built tornado-safe shelters when they know a tornado is coming.

People do not stay in their cars when a tornado strikes. Tornadoes are so powerful that they can pick up cars and throw them high into the air.

Tornadoes and nature

There are many stories of frogs falling from the sky. This is because they can get sucked up by tornadoes and then fall to the ground again when the tornado is over.

Tornadoes often blow across fields where **crops** are grown. They destroy the crops that lie in their path. A tornado's path can be over 100 metres wide.

To the rescue!

After a tornado, rescuers often find people trapped underneath flattened buildings. Ambulances take **injured** people to hospital.

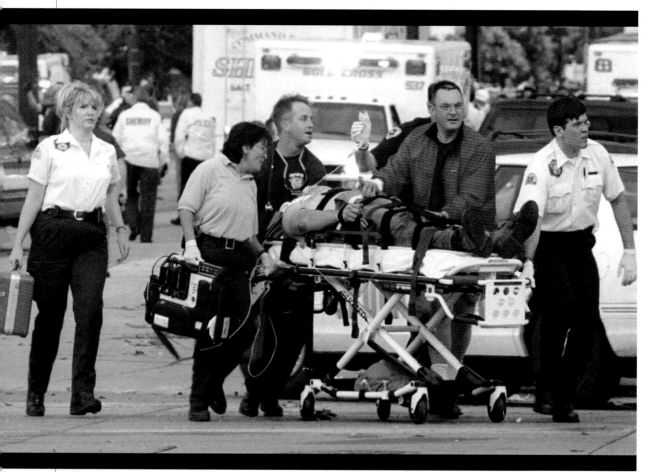

Emergency tornado shelters can protect people from tornadoes. The people's homes may still be destroyed by the tornado.

Adapting to tornadoes

People in the United States learn how to shelter from tornadoes. Here, some children are learning what to do during a tornado drill at school.

There is plenty of information about building
tornado shelters. It can be found in books or
on the Internet. People make large, strong
cupboards in their homes to hide in.

Fact file

◆ The worst tornado, that we know about, happened in Bangladesh on 2 April 1977. Around 900 people died.

◆ Tornadoes can spin at up to 480 kilometres per hour (300 miles per hour). They can travel over 350 kilometres (217 miles). Tornadoes can reach 1000 metres (1094 yards) into the sky.

◆ Scientists use invisible **radio signals** to find out if a tornado is forming. The signals bounce off **ice crystals** in the dark cloud. The signals make a pattern. If the pattern makes a hook shape, a tornado is forming.

Glossary

crops plants grown for food

debris earth and broken objects that are thrown around by the tornado

emergency services people who help us when there is a disaster. The police, ambulance and fire services are all emergency services.

funnel long, thin tube

hailstones hard balls of ice that come from thunderclouds

ice crystals tiny pieces of frozen water

injured hurt

masses huge areas or amounts of something

radio signals waves of sound that travel through the air

states large areas of a country that can make some of their own laws

waterspout huge funnel of water made when a tornado whirls over a lake, wide river or the sea

water vapour water that has changed into a gas

weather forecasters scientists who work out what weather we will get in the future

Index